Sky Beneath Your Feet

50 River Beneath 50 Ocean

Proposing Lines
Vol. 2

CHANDAN MALANA

Chandan Malana Publication House

ISBN: 9798397934817

Cover design by:
Chandan Malana

Published by
Chandan Malana
Publication House

Preface

In the ethereal realm of emotions, where love weaves its intricate patterns, the poet's pen becomes a brush that paints vivid landscapes of affection, longing, and devotion. In the tender embrace of words, hearts find solace, and souls discover their deepest desires. It is within this delicate tapestry of emotions that we embark on a journey through the pages of "Sky Beneath Your Feet," a collection of heartfelt poems and soul-stirring quotes by the talented poet, Chandan Malana.

Love, in all its splendor and complexity, is a force that transcends time and place. And during the enchanting Valentine Week, when hearts brim with ardor and passion, the author presents a captivating selection of verses and lines designed to ignite the flame of affection and pave the way for a heartfelt proposal on the cherished occasion of Propose Day.

In this compilation, Chandan Malana's words breathe life into the ethereal beauty of love, transforming mere ink on paper into an enchanting melody that resonates deep within the hearts of readers. Each poem, like a delicate petal of a blossoming flower, captures the myriad emotions that accompany the act of professing one's love. From the nervous anticipation to the exultation of hope, the author's verses encapsulate the essence of love's journey.

As you delve into the verses of "Sky Beneath Your Feet," you will be transported to a world where emotions run rampant and love weaves its intricate tapestry. The author's words will serve as a guiding light, offering solace to those who seek to express their deepest affections and propose their love to that special someone. Whether you are embarking on a new chapter or rekindling the flame of an enduring love, these poems and quotes will touch the very core of your being.

"Sky Beneath Your Feet" is a testament to the power of words, capable of capturing the essence of profound emotions in a mere handful of lines. It is an invitation to explore the depths of one's heart, to lay bare one's vulnerabilities, and to embrace the transformative power of love. With each turn of the page, you will find solace, inspiration, and a renewed sense of purpose in matters of the heart.

So, dear reader, let us embark on this journey together, as we traverse the vast expanse of emotions and immerse ourselves in the beauty of "Sky Beneath Your Feet." May these poems and quotes provide you with the courage and inspiration to express your love, and may they remind you that love, like the sky beneath your feet, is boundless and everlasting.

Message From Author

B.Sc Bioinformatics
M.Sc Microbiology
PG.Diploma In Aroma Technology

Dear Readers,

I am Chandan Malana, the author of the book "Sky Beneath Your Feet". This book has 50 poetic masterpieces on Proposing Style and 50 Proposing quotes. It is the second volume of the series "Proposing Lines".

Writing poetry has been my hobby since my school days, and it has grown into a passionate pastime. I am very proud and excited to finally share my work with you.

If you enjoy this book, I would love to publish a third volume. Please feel free to contact me at any time with your feedback, comments, and suggestions.

Thank you for your support!

Best regards,

Chandan Malana

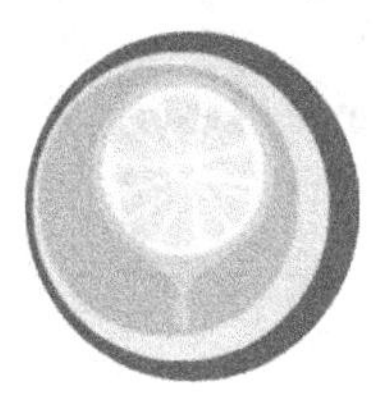

Chandan Malana Publication House

Contents

Captivated By Your Presence

When my mind wanders off in thought,

Your image is all that I've got.

And when I try to say a word,

Your name is the only one heard.

How long can I keep this inside,

These feelings I cannot subside.

Every time you cross my mind,

My heart races, I cannot unwind.

I try to hide my true intent,

But my gestures give me away, I lament.

With every smile and every touch,

I find myself falling for you so much.

I can't deny the way I feel,

My heart's desire is so real.

I'm ready now to take the chance,

To tell you, to ask you to dance.

Proposing that we take this leap,

Together we'll conquer any deep.

The love we share will light the way,

And we'll cherish every single day.

With you by my side, I am strong,

You are the lyrics to my love song.

Together we'll dance into the night,

Our love will shine oh so bright.

Let's make a vow, to never let go,

To cherish each other, and watch our love
grow.

Through every storm, and every fight,

Our love will always shine so bright.

So when I think about something new,

I know that I'll always turn to you.

My heart is yours, forevermore,

Together, we'll walk through any door.

Chandan Malana

Quote 1

"When your thoughts occupy my mind, and your name slips off my tongue, hiding my feelings seems futile. Every gesture of yours ignites a fire within me, fueling my love for you."

Chandan Malana

Confession Of Sacrificial Love: Forever Yours

My dearest love, my heart is true

I'd give up everything for you

My life, my dreams, my every breath

All for you, until my death

Without you, I am incomplete

My heart beats only for your sweet

I long to hold you in my arms

And keep you safe from all life's harms

I cannot bear to be apart

From you, the keeper of my heart

Your smile, your laugh, your gentle touch

Are all I need, I love you so much

So now I must confess my love

And pray to the heavens above

That you will hear my heartfelt plea

And share forevermore with me

I'll walk with you through life's terrain

And be with you through joy and pain

Together, we can conquer all

And make each other's spirits tall

My love, you are my one desire

My soul ignites with passion's fire

I cannot imagine life alone

For you, my heart has found its home

So please, my love, accept this ring

And all the joy and love it brings

I promise to love you forevermore

And cherish you forevermore

My dearest love, my heart is true

I'd give up everything for you

So will you take my hand in yours

And be my partner forevermore?

Chandan Malana

Quote 2

"My love for you is beyond measure. I'd lay down my life and can't bear to be without you. Today, I confess my devotion and forever pledge my heart."

Chandan Malana

Devoted Prayers For Your Happiness

I've prayed for you with ardent zeal,

My heart poured out in each appeal,

At holy sites, I knelt and prayed,

For your well-being every day.

With utmost earnestness, I've pled,

That God may bless your path ahead,

And guide you with a steady hand,

Through life's rough seas and rocky land.

In every reason for my joy,

I've asked that you may too enjoy,

The blessings that this life can bring,

And find true love that makes you sing.

My devotion to you knows no bounds,

As every day my love resounds,

With fervent prayers to heaven above,

That you may find true peace and love.

I ask that fate may lead you on,

To find the one who you belong,

And that your love will always be,

A source of strength eternally.

May every step you take in life,

Be guided by a force so bright,

And may your heart forever stay,

Filled with love in every way.

I pray that life may treat you kind,

And that your heart and soul may find,

The happiness you truly seek,

And all your dreams may come to peak.

And now, with all my heart and soul,

I make this pledge to you so bold,

To stand by you in every way,

And love you more with each passing day.

Chandan Malana

Quote 3

"My prayers for you were whispered with devotion, my requests made with utmost sincerity, every visit to God's sanctuary, a plea for your happiness in every season."

Chandan Malana

Devotion Beyond The Grave

We'll deck your heart with our heartfelt wishes,

And fill your lips with our own brand of blisses,

We vow to rescue you from the depths of the tomb,

By dedicating our very existence to your bloom.

With vibrant hues, we'll paint your heart
anew,

And spark a fire that will burn bright and
true,

We'll turn your frown upside down with our
glee,

And bring joy to your soul that's always
free.

Our desire to see you happy is
never-ending,

And we'll put in all our effort, without
pretending,

With every breath, we'll breathe life into
your veins,

And help you soar higher, breaking all your
chains.

We'll surround you with love, light, and
laughter,

And uplift you when life seems like a
disaster,

Our commitment to you is unwavering and
strong,

We'll be there for you, no matter how long.

Our devotion to you is as deep as the ocean,

And it fuels our hearts with boundless
emotion,

We'll stand by your side, come rain or shine,

And walk with you through every climb.

With every beat of our hearts, we'll sing
your name,

And we'll fan the flames of your spirit's
eternal flame,

We'll nourish your soul with our love and
care,

And guide you towards a future that's
bright and fair.

We'll be the wind beneath your wings, as
you soar,

And be the light that guides you to the
shore,

We'll hold your hand and lead you out of the
dark,

And help you build a life that's full of spark.

In this world, where nothing is certain or
sure,

We'll be the rock that you can always
endure,

We'll decorate your heart with our desires,
it's true,

And make your lips smile with our love,
forever anew.

Chandan Malana

Quote 4

"Our love will adorn your heart with its fire, and our joy will grace your lips with its desire. We promise to revive your spirit from the grave, and devote our lives to your soul's every crave."

Chandan Malana

Dreams May Amuse, But love Endures

Though dreams may bring delight,

I don't cherish them as I should,

For my love for you burns bright,

And that, my dear, is understood.

I still hold you in my heart,

With a love that will endure,

But words fail to play their part,

In expressing what is pure.

My thoughts often take flight,

And wander to worlds unknown,

But your love remains my light,

In a universe of its own.

Dreams can be a playful escape,

From the harsh realities of life,

But your love, it has no shape,

For it is pure, without strife.

Dreams may amuse, but love endures.

Though words may fail, my heart stays pure.

Although my dreams may roam,

And my mind may sometimes stray,

My love for you is my home,

And in my heart it will stay.

Words may falter and fall short,

In conveying what I truly feel,

But my love, it is a fort,

That will stand strong, with zeal.

Dreams may come and go,

But my love, it is steadfast,

And it will continue to grow,

As the years go by, and time elapse.

So, although dreams may be amusing,

And I may not express it as I should,

Know that my love for you is choosing,

To remain strong, pure, and good.

Chandan Malana

Quote 5

"Dreams may bring amusement, but my love for you is steadfast. Though I may not cherish my dreams as I should, my love for you will always endure, even if my words sometimes falter."

Chandan Malana

Endless Devotion: My Love For You

On Sunday, I shall worship thee

My love for thee, boundless and free

Not greedy, not wanting much more

Just to be thine, forevermore

Proud to call thee mine, I am

With all my heart, my love shall cram

No other desire, no other plea

Just to be with thee, endlessly

Oh, how I yearn to have thee near

To love thee, without any fear

My heart sings, a sweet melody

Proposing my love, endlessly

With each passing moment, my love grows

A love that only you truly knows

My heart beats, with passion and fire

Proposing my love, with utmost desire

On bended knee, I offer my heart

With every beat, I shall never part

My love for thee, shall never tire

Proposing my love, with a burning fire

I pledge my heart, my love to thee

For all eternity, shall we be

Together forever, hand in hand

Proposing my love, to you, my dear friend

Oh, how I long to hold thee tight

To kiss thee, under the moonlight

My love for thee, shall never fade

Proposing my love, with every shade

So, my love, will you be mine?

Together, forever, shall we entwine?

My heart, my love, I offer to thee

Proposing my love, for all to see.

Chandan Malana

Quote 6

"I desire to worship and love you with all my heart, without greed or excess. My only wish is to have you as mine in every moment, and to make you proud."

Chandan Malana

Endless Longing: The Madness Of Remembering You

What label fits this madness of mine,

Restless heart now starts to whine,

Passion stirred, recalls you divine,

Oh, what name do I give this sign?

My thoughts propose to call it love,

A feeling pure, like wings of dove,

Yet doubts creep in, make me shove,

Do I dare call it love thereof?

This restlessness, a constant ache,

A hunger for you, no mistake,

Desire fuels, keeps me awake,

What should I name this thirsting stake?

Perhaps infatuation it be,

A fleeting fancy, I now see,

But no, it lingers constantly,

A love that yearns unceasingly.

A madness, yes, but not of ill,

A longing that I cannot still,

My heartstrings tugged against my will,

What name to give, it baffles still.

This passion for you, an obsession,

An all-consuming possession,

An addiction, without exception,

What term suits this great confession?

Some may call it crazy or wild,

But to me, it's like a child,

Pure and innocent, undefiled,

What name to give, it's got me beguiled.

In the end, I'll simply say this,

My heart for you, it cannot miss,

A love that's true, a love that's bliss,

No matter what name, it's you I'll kiss.

Chandan Malana

Quote 7

"Amidst this madness, my heart's ache begs for a name, as my passion remembers you every moment, but what words do I use to convey such a flame?"

Chandan Malana

Ensnared By Love: A Transformative Journey

When love is spoken, we'll ensnare your heart,

And take you to realms that are pure art,

Our wild passion will make you feel alive,

As we transform your world with love and drive.

In moments of solitude, we'll be by your
side,

Decorating your surroundings with love's
pride,

Our presence will fill your heart with cheer,

As we wrap you up in love so dear.

We'll bring a smile to your lips so bright,

And chase away all your fears and fright,

With us by your side, you'll never feel alone,

As our love for you will forever be shown.

When you finally confess your love so pure,

We'll be there waiting with love to endure,

Our hearts will beat as one with love
unbound,

As we cherish every moment that we've
found.

We'll be crazy in love, just like we'll make
you,

As our passion ignites and sparks anew,

Our love will be the light that guides your
way,

And fills your heart with love each day.

We'll dance under the stars, hand in hand,

As we pledge our love to forever stand,

With each breath we take, our love will
grow,

As we embrace each other in love's warm
glow.

Our love will be a symphony of sweet sound,

As we dance to the rhythm of love's
profound,

Together we'll make a perfect melody,

As our love story unfolds beautifully.

So, if you're ready to take a chance,

And join us in love's eternal dance,

We promise to love you with all our heart,

And never let our love ever fall apart.

Chandan Malana

Quote 8

"When you express your love, we'll turn your world upside down, filling it with joy and crazy love. We'll wait for your confession and decorate your solitude with love's gathering."

Chandan Malana

Eternal Gem Of Love

Your scent drifts by on evening's breeze,

A fragrance that my soul doth seize,

Your love's sparkle forever glows,

A light that always brightly shows.

In our hearts your memories stay,

A treasure we won't give away,

For you are like a precious gem,

A love that time cannot condemn.

My life is richer for your love,

A gift bestowed from up above,

And so I offer you this ring,

My heart to yours forever cling.

With each passing day I see,

The beauty that you bring to me,

Your grace and kindness fill my heart,

And never shall we be apart.

My love for you will never fade,

A flame that burns with passion's shade,

For in your eyes I see my soul,

And in your arms I am made whole.

So take this ring and be my wife,

Together we'll share a precious life,

And all the world will surely know,

That we are one, our love aglow.

Through all life's storms we'll stand
together,

And brave the trials we may weather,

For in our hearts we know the truth,

That love is strong, and love will soothe.

So let us join in love's embrace,

And journey forth with grace and grace,

For you are the second name of my life,

My love, my partner, my cherished wife.

Chandan Malana

Quote 9

"You are the essence that lingers in the air, the glimmer that illuminates love's affair. Your memories reside deep within our hearts, for you are the very soul of my life, never to depart."

Chandan Malana

Eternally Together: A Promise Of Forever Love

My heart sings a song of love for you,

A melody that's pure and true,

I cannot bear the thought of parting ways,

Nor do I want to count my tear-filled days.

My soul longs to be by your side,

In your warm embrace, I want to reside,

I never want to let you go,

Or face a life of sorrow.

My love, I vow to stay with you,

Till the end of time, forever true,

I promise to hold your hand,

And walk with you through every land.

Life without you is a bleak picture,

A world devoid of color and texture,

I want to be with you, my dear,

And chase away every trace of fear.

Let us face the world together,

Hand in hand, like birds of a feather,

Let our love be a shining light,

Guiding us through the darkest night.

My heart beats with the rhythm of love,

A symphony played from up above,

I want to be with you, my love,

And cherish every moment thereof.

I cannot imagine life without you,

My love, I am proposing anew,

Will you be mine forevermore?

And share with me an eternity to adore?

Together, we'll weather every storm,

And keep our love forever warm,

Neither loss nor tears will come to be,

As long as I'm with you, my love, for
eternity.

Chandan Malana

Quote 10

"I never want to say goodbye or shed tears in your memory, for as long as I live, I want to hold onto you tightly and cherish every moment with you."

Chandan Malana

Everlasting Promise: A Hand To Hold

Our promise to you, unbreakable and true,

We'll stand by your side, no matter what you do,

Even if you forget, and move far away,

We'll come and find you, without delay.

Our love for you, will never fade,

We'll never abandon you, or let you be
swayed,

Through thick and thin, we'll always be
near,

To help and support you, and chase away
your fear.

We'll catch your hand, and hold it tight,

Guide you through darkness, into the light,

With open hearts, and arms outstretched,

We'll be there for you, without regret.

Our bond with you, will always endure,

Even if you falter, and are unsure,

We'll lift you up, and give you hope,

Help you to cope, and find your way to cope.

Our words may be few, but our actions will
show,

That our promise to you, will never go,

We'll be your rock, your anchor, your shield,

Your refuge from the world, your safe place
to yield.

We'll walk with you, every step of the way,

Never faltering, never led astray,

Our love for you, will always be strong,

A bond that will last, all lifelong.

We propose to you, this heartfelt vow,

To always be there, through here and now,

To catch your hand, and never let go,

Through life's highs and lows, our love will
grow.

So take our hand, and come with us,

Together we'll walk, without any fuss,

Our promise to you, will never subside,

We'll be there for you, with love and pride.

Chandan Malana

Quote 11

"Our promise to you is unwavering and true, we'll be there for you no matter what you do. Even if you wander far and wide, we'll catch your hand again and stand by your side."

Chandan Malana

Expressing Agreement Beyond Words

Agreement need not rely on words,

Emotions of the heart go unheard,

But fear not, for there is a way,

To convey what you need to say.

The voice may falter or remain still,

But the heart can speak with a will,

And in the eyes, a tale is told,

Of what the heart may try to hold.

Love is not bound to spoken phrase,

Nor the words we often raise,

For in a simple gaze or stare,

The truth of love is laid out bare.

The heart's emotions, pure and true,

Are felt by the one who loves you,

And though words may seem to be,

The only way to set them free.

The eyes can tell a story too,

Of love that's strong, and love that's new,

And through a simple look or glance,

You can express your heart's romance.

So if the words are hard to find,

Don't let it weigh upon your mind,

For love will find a way to show,

And in your eyes, it soon will glow.

Let your heart lead the way,

And let your eyes do the talking today,

For in the end, it's love that wins,

And the heart that always begins.

So let your eyes and heart unite,

And let your love shine bright,

For words may come and words may go,

But the language of love will always flow.

Chandan Malana

Quote 12

"Agreement is not bound by words, the heart's voice and eyes tell the tale of love, for true love needs not rely on spoken phrase."

Chandan Malana

Expressions of the Heart: Our Story Unfolds

Come take my hand and come with me,

We'll journey to a distant land, you'll see,

Where we can share the tale of our hearts,

And reveal the secrets of our inner parts.

We'll wander through the fields and
streams,

And bask in the sun's warm, golden beams,

With each step we take, we'll be proposing,

A future where our love keeps blossoming.

Our eyes will meet and speak of love,

And our hearts will beat like gentle doves,

For in this moment, we'll be free,

To express our love, so honestly.

We'll climb up hills and mountains high,

And gaze upon the endless sky,

As we tell our story, through every rhyme,

Our love will grow, like a rose in its prime.

Our hands will hold and never let go,

As we walk along this path we've come to
know,

And with each step, we'll be proposing,

A life of love, forever imposing.

The sun will set, and the moon will rise,

And we'll still be here, side by side,

We'll tell our story, with every word,

And the magic of our love will be heard.

We'll whisper sweet nothings in each other's
ears,

And laugh at all our silly fears,

For in this moment, we'll be proposing,

A lifetime of love, forever composing.

So come along with me, my dear,

To a place where love has no fear,

We'll tell the whole story, through our
expressions and words,

And our love will be forever heard.

Chandan Malana

Quote 13

"Let's take a journey to a place unknown, Where words and expressions become our own, We'll tell our story, a tale so true, And explain what our eyes can't construe."

Chandan Malana

Eyes and Hearts: A Love That Sets Us Free

Gaze into my eyes and know,

Our hearts are ready to grow,

When they meet, we'll be set free,

A love that's pure, just you and me.

Embrace the joys of life, my dear,

With your love, there's nothing to fear,

Let our hearts intertwine and blend,

A love that lasts, until the end.

With every look, we'll see it's true,

Our love will always renew,

Just declare it loud and clear,

And we'll share a love that's sincere.

Let's hold each other close and tight,

And bask in love's sweet delight,

Our hearts entwined, we'll face the world,

Together, our love will unfurl.

In your eyes, I see my heart,

A bond that can't be torn apart,

Our love will conquer any strife,

Together, we'll embrace a joyful life.

With every beat, our hearts align,

A love that's pure, and truly divine,

Let's take a chance, and seize the day,

Together, we'll find a love that'll stay.

Our love will shine like the brightest star,

No matter where we are,

Let's hold each other's hands and see,

What our love can truly be.

So look into my eyes, my love,

And see the blessings from above,

Our hearts will meet, and we'll be whole,

A love that's pure, and truly bold.

Chandan Malana

Quote 14

"Unlock the power of love, meet eyes with eyes and hearts with hearts. Embrace the joys of the world and declare your love, for in that moment, true freedom is found."

Chandan Malana

Follow The Beat Of My Hearts

Oh my dear companion, lend me your ear

As I speak of a path we could steer

Listen closely to the beating of my heart

For it yearns for a love that will never depart

Together, we can choose our way

With every step, our love will never sway

Believe in us, and take a chance

Let us embark on this sweet romance

Take my hand, let me lead the way

Towards a love that will never fray

Let our hearts be intertwined

As we walk this path so divine

The future may be uncertain, my love

But together we can rise above

Let's build a life filled with laughter and
bliss

And seal it with a tender kiss

Our love is like a garden, let it grow

Nurtured by our love, it will surely glow

We'll water it with tears of joy and sorrow

And watch it bloom for many tomorrows

With you by my side, my heart is full

Overflowing with love, like a tidal pool

Let's make a promise, you and me

To love each other for eternity

Our love is like a precious gem

More valuable than any diadem

Let's cherish it with all our might

And make it shine forever bright

So my dear companion, what do you say?

Will you join me on this path today?

Let's journey together, hand in hand

And love each other, as only we can.

Chandan Malana

Quote 15

"Trust the rhythm of my heart, dear Companion. Let us carve our own path and at every step, our love will guide us. If doubts still linger, take a chance and witness the magic we can create."

Chandan Malana

Forever & Always, Only You

With every breath that I take, my love for you grows

And in my heart, only your love forever glows

I swear to you, my sweet and beloved one

That my love for you will never be outdone

In your eyes, I see a future so bright

And I'll do all I can to make it just right

I swear to you, my dear, my heart is true

This love will never be for anyone new

I'll love you in every season, in every way

From the first light of dawn until the end of
the day

I swear to you, my love, I'll always be here

Through every joy and every tear

No matter where our path may lead

Together, we'll conquer any deed

I swear by our love, it will never fade

And through every challenge, we'll never be swayed

I'll stand by your side, through thick and thin

Through every battle that we may win

I swear to you, my heart is yours

Forever and always, through all life's tours

My love for you is a fire that never dies

And with each passing day, it only
multiplies

I swear to you, my sweet and precious one

That our love will never be outdone

Let this love be a shining light

Guiding us through both day and night

I swear to you, my love, I'll always be true

And forever, my heart belongs to only you

So here, in this moment, I make this vow

To love you forever, here and now

I swear by our love, it will never end

And I ask you, my love, will you be mine
until the very end?

Chandan Malana

Quote 16

"My love for you is pure and true. No one else will ever do. I swear by our love, it's only you. Forever and always, I will be true."

Chandan Malana

Forever Bound: A Love That Cannot Be Torn

The rose within my heart did grow,

A symbol of our love's sweet flow,

Through days and nights of passion's glow,

Our bond did thrive and ever grow.

In slumber's grasp, I dreamed of thee,

A world of love and harmony,

Where nothing else could ever be,

But you and I, eternally.

I asked you, "How much do you love?"

A question sent from up above,

And with a tender, heartfelt shove,

You said, "We'll die without your love."

Proposing now, my heart beats fast,

The moment here has come at last,

To ask the question that will last,

Forevermore, until the past.

With trembling hands, I take your own,

And vow to love and make a home,

Where we will never be alone,

Together, always, we'll be known.

The ring I give, a symbol true,

Of all the love I have for you,

A promise made to see it through,

And always hold our love anew.

You say yes, and tears do flow,

As we begin our life's great show,

With love as our guide, we'll go,

And let our hearts forever grow.

The rose in the book of heart was ours,

Through all life's trials and all its powers,

We'll cherish it as love empowers,

Our journey together, until the final hours.

Chandan Malana

Quote 17

"Our hearts were bound by a rose in our book, In dreams, our love was all it took. And when we asked, 'How much do you love me?' The answer was, 'We will die without thee.'"

Chandan Malana

Glimpses Of Love In Her Amazing Eyes

Her eyes, a sight so rare,

Speak volumes beyond compare,

Each glance a tale to unfold,

My heart, by their beauty, behold.

Like windows to her soul,

Her gaze, a treasure to behold,

It weaves tales of love and grace,

My heart dances at its pace.

Sometimes they sparkle like the sun,

Other times they glisten and run,

But always, they reveal her truth,

And in them, I find my eternal youth.

Her lowered lashes, oh how they confess,

A love that fills me with sweet caress,

My heart races at every blink,

As her eyes, my soul doth sink.

They captivate me with their charm,

A love so pure, it can disarm,

Their beauty, a sight to propose,

In them, my heart forever glows.

With every gaze, they steal my breath,

A love so true, it can conquer death,

My heart beats for her and her alone,

As her eyes, my soul they own.

They tell a story without words,

Of a love that's pure, like singing birds,

In them, my heart finds its home,

And I never want to be alone.

Her eyes, they are truly amazing,

A love so deep, it's worth proposing,

In them, I find my heart's delight,

As I pledge my love, forever bright.

Chandan Malana

Quote 18

"Her eyes, a masterpiece of expression, telling tales of love and life with every glance. My heart races in those moments, when her lowered lashes reveal her deepest emotions."

Chandan Malana

Heart's Craving

My heart yearns to love you more,

To express feelings deep at core,

Ever since I laid eyes on you,

My heart has known what it should do.

Oh, beloved, you fill me with delight,

Your presence makes everything right,

My heart desires nothing more,

Than to be with you forevermore.

In my dreams, I see you by my side,

As my heart's love I cannot hide,

I want to hold you close and near,

And whisper sweet words in your ear.

Let me propose my love to you,

With every breath, my love is true,

Together, we can walk life's path,

With love as our guide, we'll never look
back.

My heart beats faster when you're near,

It's clear to me, you are my dear,

I want to spend each moment with you,

With a love that's strong and true.

My love for you will never fade,

With each passing day, it's only made,

Stronger and more passionate too,

My heart belongs to only you.

So, my beloved, please hear my plea,

Be with me now and forever be,

Let's take this journey together, hand in
hand,

With a love that will forever stand.

My heart wants to love you more,

And express the love it has in store,

My beloved, will you be mine,

And let our hearts entwine?

Chandan Malana

Quote 19

"From the moment I saw you, my heart knew its purpose - to love you fiercely and express its adoration for you every day."

Chandan Malana

Heart's Inquiry: Will You Hold My Hand and Love Me?

As the stars twinkle above,

My heart's overflowing with love,

I want to ask you something so true,

Will you share your life with me, will you?

Let's take a walk hand in hand,

Together we'll build a love so grand,

My heart beats with joy and glee,

As I ask you to spend forever with me.

Close your eyes and listen to your heart,

I promise we'll never be apart,

Let me be the one to cherish and adore,

And I'll love you more and more.

I'll be your shelter from the storm,

A love so pure, it'll keep you warm,

Just say the word and we'll start anew,

Together we'll make all our dreams come
true.

Do you see a future with me?

A life full of love and harmony,

Let's make a promise to never part,

And hold each other's hand with all our
heart.

I want to be the one by your side,

Through the ups and downs, we'll ride,

Together we'll face life's every test,

And our love will always be the best.

So take my hand and say yes,

Let our love be the ultimate success,

I'll always be here to love and support,

And cherish you in every way, in every sort.

Let's embark on this journey together,

A love so strong, it'll last forever,

I'll be your partner, your lover, your friend,

And our love story will never end.

Chandan Malana

Quote 20

"Listen to the whispers of your heart, as you close your eyes and ask - do you like me, do you want to be mine? Will you hold my hand and love me? For in those answers lies the beauty of a love story waiting to unfold."

Chandan Malana

Love Can't Be Defined

Don't inquire of me what love may be,

Would you trust me if I just decree?

Words can't express the passion you'll see,

Put it to the test and you'll agree.

I could speak of hearts and butterflies,

But words are just words, devoid of ties,

It's a feeling that you can't compromise,

Give it a chance, and love will arise.

It's not something that can be defined,

Like the wind, it can't be confined,

But once you sense it, it's all entwined,

A bond that forever will bind.

It's not only sweet and joyous bliss,

It's pain and tears that you can't dismiss,

A rollercoaster of emotion, hit or miss,

Yet, it's worth the ride, don't you miss.

It's a leap of faith, a wild gamble,

A chance to unravel, unravel and ramble,

In unknown territories, ready to scramble,

It's a journey, not just a mere sample.

It's a burning fire, a glowing flame,

A constant passion, it's never the same,

An endless adventure, without any blame,

It's a love that forever will proclaim.

It's not just for the young and bold,

But for the old, and for the hearted cold,

For all who seek a love that can't be sold,

It's an eternal flame that can't be
controlled.

So don't ask me what love is all about,

Give it a shot, that's all I can tout,

For in the end, you'll never have a doubt,

It's the greatest feeling, without any clout.

Chandan Malana

Quote 21

"Love can't be defined by words alone. Believe me, it's worth experiencing. Don't ask, just give it a chance. You'll know what it is when you feel it."

Chandan Malana

Love Surpasses Words

Love is a force that knows no tongue,

Its power so great, it can't be undone,

In tears and smiles, it finds its voice,

Expressions that make our hearts rejoice.

No language barrier can hold it back,

It breaks down walls, fills every lack,

It's a universal tongue that all can speak,

A flame that ignites the coldest of weeks.

When love is found, it's a precious treasure,

A bond that lasts beyond measure,

To hold it close, to cherish each moment,

Is to experience a love so potent.

Love's power is immense, it's true,

It fills our hearts, makes us anew,

It's a force that knows no bounds,

A symphony that never resounds.

Love's tears are bittersweet,

Its smiles make our hearts skip a beat,

It speaks louder than any words could ever
express,

And brings us a happiness that's hard to
suppress.

Cherish the love that you have found,

For it's a blessing that's truly profound,

Not everyone gets to experience its glow,

So hold it close and never let go.

Propose to love with all your heart,

And let it guide you from the start,

Through thick and thin, it will remain,

A love that transcends all pain.

So let your love be the light that shines,

A bond that endures through all the hard times,

For love is a language that needs no translation,

A blessing that fills our hearts with elation.

Chandan Malana

Quote 22

"Love surpasses words; tears and smiles speak volumes. Cherish it, for it's a rare blessing not granted to all. "

Chandan Malana

Love Uncontained: Embracing Life's Journey

Love unbridled cannot be contained,

Its power and passion cannot be restrained.

Like a wild fire that spreads with zeal,

It consumes everything in its path, real.

Life's journey is not always smooth,

It's full of twists and turns, that's the truth.

Like hair tangled beyond repair,

Some things in life cannot be repaired.

But love has a way to make us whole,

To mend our hearts, to heal our soul.

So hold the hand of the one who cares,

Together you can conquer any fears.

Life moves on, it doesn't wait,

For what is done, it's too late.

But with love by your side,

You'll find the strength to take in stride.

Love that scatters is hard to regain,

Like shattered glass, it leaves a stain.

But if you're willing to try,

Love can mend what once did die.

Propose to your love, don't wait too long,

Time is fleeting, it won't be long.

Take the leap and ask for their hand,

Together you'll make a life so grand.

Love is the glue that binds us tight,

It gives us wings to take in flight.

Through life's ups and downs, we'll soar,

With love as our foundation, we'll want for
more.

So cherish the love that you've found,

Don't let it go, it's so profound.

Hold on tight and never let go,

Together you'll conquer, that's for sure.

Chandan Malana

Quote 23

"Love, once scattered, cannot be confined;
Life, unlike hair, can't be combed to rewind.
Grasp the hand of one who loves you true;
For life never halts for what's already due."

Chandan Malana

Love, Like Morning Dew

Our love is tender, gentle and pure,

A tale as fragile as a porcelain lure,

She is the sun that brightens my day,

In her arms, forever I'll stay.

Our hearts beat in perfect sync,

With every touch, our souls interlink,

In this love, we both find bliss,

A sweet embrace, sealed with a kiss.

It's a love so rare and divine,

A bond as strong as the grapevine,

She is my world, my everything,

My heart's desire, my eternal spring.

Her love is like the morning dew,

Glistening, shining, fresh and new,

It nourishes my soul with every drop,

And makes my heart leap and hop.

In her eyes, I see a reflection of me,

A love that is real, honest and free,

Together, we'll weather every storm,

And emerge victorious, forever warm.

Our love is a song that never ends,

A symphony of hearts that blend,

It's a tale of two hearts that beat as one,

A love that's pure, strong and never done.

I ask her now, with all my heart,

To take my hand and never be apart,

Together, we'll travel life's winding road,

With love as our compass, our constant
abode.

It's a love so fragile and true,

A tale as delicate as the morning dew,

But with her by my side, I am complete,

And in our love, we both truly meet.

Chandan Malana

Quote 24

"Love, like morning dew, is fragile and delicate, yet so true. When we are together, we both shine with a light that brightens even the darkest of days."

Chandan Malana

Love's Paradoxical Dilemma

We keep our feelings buried deep inside,

Afraid of the reaction they might provide,

The thought of their answer fills us with dread,

A "yes" would mean joy, but "no" would bring tears shed.

Our love remains hidden, concealed and
repressed,

A secret kept hidden, within our chest,

For the fear of rejection looms overhead,

A risk too great, we'd rather not be led.

The possibility of happiness excites,

A world of love and passion, we could ignite,

But what if their answer is not what we
crave,

And our hearts become broken, destined to
cave.

We long to express the depth of our love,

But the fear of rejection is all we can think
of,

We wonder if they feel the same way too,

Or if our feelings are one-sided, what will
we do?

Proposing our love seems too big a feat,

A daunting task that we cannot defeat,

We dream of a future where we are
together,

But the fear of rejection could last forever.

The thought of their response, makes us anxious inside,

Will our love be reciprocated or simply denied,

If they say yes, our hearts will fill with glee,

But if they say no, our hearts will break instantly.

We wish we could express our love with ease,

Without the fear of what their answer may be,

But until then, we'll keep our feelings concealed,

Hoping someday, our love will be revealed.

So, we continue to love from afar,

Hoping that one day we'll get to be where they are,

And muster up the courage to finally propose,

Our love for them, we cannot keep it enclosed.

Chandan Malana

Quote 25

"We keep our love hidden, afraid of their reply, A "yes" would bring joy, a "no" would make us cry, Our hearts remain silent, for the fear is too great, The risk of rejection, we cannot contemplate."

Chandan Malana

Loyal Friends: Our Promise To Hold Your Hand

Our vow to you, forever strong,

We'll be your anchor all life long,

Even if you stray and roam,

We'll seek you out and guide you home.

Our pledge to stay by your side,

Through every storm and every tide,

No matter where your path may wind,

We'll be the constant, true and kind.

If ever you should slip away,

We'll come and lead you back each day,

And if you feel lost and alone,

We'll offer comfort, like a warm home.

With open arms, we'll always be,

The steadfast friend you need to see,

And if you ever feel unsure,

We'll be the light to guide you pure.

Our promise rings forever true,

We'll cherish all the time with you,

And through each high and every low,

We'll be the love that helps you grow.

No matter what the future brings,

We'll be the song that always sings,

And with each step that you take,

We'll be the hand to help you make.

So take our hand and hold it tight,

We'll never let you out of sight,

And with our love, we'll pave the way,

For brighter skies on every day.

This promise, now and evermore,

Is ours to keep, and to adore,

And with this bond, we now propose,

A friendship that forever grows.

Chandan Malana

Quote 26

"We promise to always stand by you, through thick and thin. Even if you wander off and forget about us, we'll be there to hold your hand and guide you back home."

Chandan Malana

Melodic Love: A River That Never Withers

Come closer, my dear, and connect with me

Like the thread of fate that ties destiny

Let's be like Ranjha and Heer, loyal and true

Our love, like theirs, forever anew

I remember you always, day and night

My thoughts of you, a constant delight

Let's join our lives, and never be apart

With you by my side, I have a full heart

Like a melody that stays in my head

Your love is the song that I always tread

Let's walk this path, hand in hand, forever

Our love, like a river, will never wither

I know sometimes I may stumble and fall

But with your love, I'll rise above it all

So if hiccups come, please forgive me in
advance

Our love will withstand any circumstance

Let's make a vow to love and cherish

Our love, like a flame, will never perish

I propose to you, my love, with all my heart

Let's embark on this journey, a new start

Together we'll face the highs and the lows

Our love, like a rose, will continue to grow

Let's create memories that we'll treasure

Our love will be a source of pleasure

Like the stars that twinkle in the sky

Our love will never fade, it will never die

Let's embrace each other, and never let go

Our love, like the sun, will always glow

So, my love, please say yes to me

Together we'll make a beautiful history

Let's be each other's destiny, forevermore

Our love will be an unbreakable rapport.

Chandan Malana

Quote 27

"Your love, a melody that never fades, like a river that never withers. With you, I'll rise above every fall, our love will withstand it all."

Chandan Malana

My Heart's Sole Image: Needing You More Than the World

Today every second is a delight,

In my heart, you're the only sight,

Amidst the chaos and the noise,

You're the only one who brings me poise.

The world may speak of a thousand things,

But my heart with only your image rings,

Your love is all I ever need,

In this life, it's you I want to lead.

The beauty of the world cannot compare,

To the love that we both share,

No matter what the world may say,

I'll love you more with each passing day.

The sun may set and the stars may rise,

But my heart for you never dies,

You complete me in every way,

Will you be mine forever and a day?

I promise to cherish you with all my heart,

Together we'll never be apart,

With you, I find my true purpose,

You're my forever, my one true bliss.

Our love is like a rose in bloom,

Forever fragrant, never to consume,

A love that's pure and never fades,

In your embrace, my soul finds shades.

Let's walk hand in hand, side by side,

Together, we'll cross life's wild tide,

In this journey of love, let's unite,

My heart beats only for you, day and night.

So, my love, with this poem I propose,

To love and cherish you, with all my lows
and highs,

Will you be mine, forever and more?

I promise to love you like never before.

Chandan Malana

Quote 28

"Every moment is a precious sight, in my heart, you shine so bright. Amidst the world's chaos and fuss, my need for you surpasses all else."

Chandan Malana

My Love Is True, Despite Temptation's Call

Although my dreams may sweep me off my feet,

I don't let their allure make my heart skip a beat.

For even though they tempt me with their charm,

I know in reality they'll do me harm.

Despite their pull, I don't fall in love with
dreams,

For they're but illusions, not as real as it
seems.

They may bring me joy, but it's fleeting at
best,

And I know that in the end, they'll leave me
unimpressed.

Instead, my heart belongs to you alone,

For you're the one who's made my heart a
home.

Your love is true, and it fills me up each day,

And in my heart, it's where I long to stay.

Though I may not express it all the time,

My love for you remains, a constant, steady rhyme.

It beats within my heart, a song that's never ending,

And to you, my love, it's always extending.

I may not shower you with flowery prose,

Or write you poems that make your heart
flutter and glow,

But know that my love for you is deep and
true,

And it will always be, no matter what we go
through.

With every passing day, my love for you
grows,

And in my heart, it's a feeling that
overflows.

It fills me up with joy and makes me feel
alive,

And in your arms, it's where I want to
thrive.

So although dreams may come and go,

My love for you will continue to grow.

It's a love that's pure, and it's here to stay,

And in your heart, I hope it finds its way.

My love, will you do me the honor,

Of being mine, now and forever,

For you're the one I want by my side,

My partner, my love, my constant guide.

Chandan Malana

Quote 29

"I am tempted by dreams' allure, but my heart remains true. Though my love for you is steadfast, my lips fail to express it."

Chandan Malana

Naming Our Love

Let's not keep our love hidden away,

Instead, let's give it a name today,

Let's shout it out for all to hear,

So everyone knows that we hold it dear.

Our love is like a beautiful song,

That's been playing in our hearts for so
long,

Let's give it a gift that's just as sweet,

Something that will make our love
complete.

Before our hearts get filled with strifc,

Let's take a moment to cherish our life,

Let's make our desires known and clear,

And celebrate our love with a cheer.

We've been holding back for too long,

Our love is too precious to keep it wrong,

Let's propose to each other with all our
might,

And make this evening a beautiful sight.

Let's fill the air with love and joy,

And let our hearts be each other's toy,

Let's dance and sing until the dawn,

And make this night one we'll always fawn.

Let's give our love a chance to shine,

And show the world that it's divine,

Let's hold each other close and tight,

And let our love be the brightest light.

Let's forget about the worries and fears,

And focus on each other, wipe away the
tears,

Let's make this night a night to remember,

And vow to love each other forever.

So, let's give a silent love a name today,

And propose to each other in a beautiful way,

Let's make our desires known and true,

And celebrate our love, just me and you.

Chandan Malana

Quote 30

"Let us not keep our love silent and unnamed, but instead, let's give it a beautiful gift and give voice to our desires. For in doing so, we can create a pleasant evening and prevent any future upset."

Chandan Malana

Noble Love: A Heart's Offering

If you want to give your heart away,

Choose someone noble, don't just give it astray,

It's not a temple offering for all to take,

Find someone deserving, for love's sake.

Proposing your heart is a sacred vow,

Not to be given to just anyone somehow,

Seek a heart that beats with a noble beat,

One that will treasure your love, so sweet.

Love is not a game, nor a fleeting affair,

It's a commitment to cherish and to care,

Give your heart to someone who'll
appreciate,

Your love, your passion, your every trait.

Don't give your heart to someone without
measure,

Choose someone who brings you joy and
pleasure,

Someone who'll stand by you through thick
and thin,

And cherish the love that you'll bring in.

Find someone who's kind and true,

Whose love for you will always renew,

Someone who'll be there in times of need,

And whose love for you will never recede.

Choose someone with a heart of gold,

Whose love for you will never grow old,

Someone who'll cherish every moment,

And love you, whether or not you're present.

Remember, your heart is a precious gift,

Don't give it away to someone who'll just
lift,

Your spirits for a moment, then let you
down,

Find someone noble, with a heart to
astound.

So, if you're proposing your heart to
someone,

Make sure it's to someone who's not just
anyone,

Find someone who'll love you through thick
and thin,

And cherish the love that you bring in.

Chandan Malana

Quote 31

"Offer your heart to a noble soul, not as a temple offering for all to behold, for true love is a sacred gift, to be cherished and treasured, not just distributed to anyone."

Chandan Malana

Picture In Your Heart

In your heart lies a picture so true,

Of someone who makes your heart anew,

Yet your feelings are yet to pursue,

No better day than today, it's overdue.

Their image lingers in your mind,

The thought of them, oh how it's kind,

But your heart is still confined,

Open up, let your feelings unwind.

Don't let fear make your love subside,

Confess your heart, take it in stride,

With them by your side, you'll feel alive,

Propose today, let love arrive.

Life's too short to hold back,

Take a leap, don't fall off track,

With them, you'll feel on the right track,

Let your heart speak, let love attack.

The future is a mystery untold,

But with them, your heart will unfold,

Take a chance, let your love be bold,

Propose today, watch your love take hold.

Don't wait for the perfect moment,

For love doesn't come with an omen,

With them, your heart will be atonement,

Propose today, love will be potent.

It's time to take a step forward,

Don't let love be left ignored,

With them, your life will be adored,

Propose today, let love be explored.

So, if someone's picture in your heart rings
true,

And you've yet to express your love anew,

Take the chance, let your heart come
through,

Propose today, love will ensue.

Chandan Malana

Quote 32

"Let not the picture in your heart fade away, for love unexpressed is a debt left unpaid. If their image lingers and your feelings are true, seize the day and make your heart known, for there is no better day than today to let your love bloom."

Chandan Malana

Priceless Love: Beyond Words and Tears

Words may falter, fail to show,

Emotions deep, that overflow,

In tears that stream and freely flow,

Love defying language, we all know.

How can mere words hope to convey,

All the love we feel each day,

When the heart bursts in a beautiful way,

And words can't catch up or have their say.

But still we try, to find the phrase,

That will our feelings best portray,

To let our love be heard and praised,

And make it clear in all our ways.

Yet when love is true and pure,

Words can't contain it, that's for sure,

For love is meant to be felt more,

Then what mere language can explore.

So when you find love in your life,

Value it more than gold or strife,

Hold it close, let it thrive,

For not all are blessed with love so rife.

And if you have found that special one,

Who makes your heart dance and sing with fun,

Treasure them, like the setting sun,

Cherish them, until the day is done.

For love is rare and hard to find,

And when it's there, it's like a bind,

That keeps two hearts, forever entwined,

In a love that is truly one of a kind.

So let the tears of joy flow free,

When words can't capture what you see,

In a love that's pure and meant to be,

An endless bond for all eternity.

Chandan Malana

Quote 33

"Love is the emotion that transcends language, it's tears and smiles speak louder than any words could ever express. So if you find love, cherish it dearly, for it is a blessing not bestowed upon all."

Chandan Malana

Self-Mastery: The Power Within

Those who mourn and try to jest,

May find their pain is unimpressed,

For laughter cannot bring relief,

To wounds that ache beyond belief.

Waves crashing on the shore,

Cannot be stilled forevermore,

Their tumultuous force won't be tamed,

As they surge on, unashamed.

We are the architects of our fate,

The masters of our own estate,

No other can control our mind,

Or the destiny that we will find.

You can't force someone to be,

A master of their destiny,

For true autonomy comes from within,

Not from another's discipline.

It's important to lend a hand,

To those who struggle to understand,

That they hold the power to be great,

And it's up to them to create their fate.

We all have a voice to express,

Our thoughts and feelings to address,

It's up to us to use it well,

And let our inner light dispel.

Proposing that we all take charge,

Of our lives, and not be in a mirage,

Believe in ourselves, and take control,

Of the direction that we will unroll.

So let us not wait to be told,

That we are strong, and not to fold,

For we are the makers of our own story,

And the true authors of our own glory.

Chandan Malana

Quote 34

"Laughter cannot heal grief, waves cannot be tamed, true autonomy comes from within. One must choose to become their own, not be told to do so."

Chandan Malana

Silent Lips, Restless Heart: A Love Without Limits

My lips long to keep silent and still,

But my heart beats fast, against my will,

For within me, a love burns bright and true,

Unbounded and endless, solely for you.

I yearn to keep my feelings unspoken,

To leave them hidden, unprovoked and
unbroken,

Yet my heart, restless and full of desire,

Urges my lips to speak, like a raging fire.

This love, oh, it knows no bounds or limits,

It is pure, raw, and free from any gimmicks,

It exists solely to make you feel adored,

To sweep you up and carry you forward.

I know not how to convey this emotion,

My words seem to fall short of its devotion,

But still, I'll try to capture it in my verse,

To let you know this love, it's a universe.

A world where joy and happiness reign,

Where hearts are full, and there's no pain,

Where love thrives in all its splendor,

And every moment feels like a grand
adventure.

So I propose this love to you, my dear,

With every fiber of my being, sincere and
clear,

To take your hand and walk this path with
me,

To embrace this love, and let our hearts be
free.

For though my lips may sometimes falter,

And my words may sometimes seem to
alter,

My love for you will always remain constant,

A flame that burns bright, pure and vibrant.

So let us keep our hearts open and wide,

And let this love take us on a thrilling ride,

For with you by my side, I know we can
soar,

To heights we've never reached before.

Chandan Malana

Quote 35

"Silent lips may hide a love without limits, but a restless heart will eventually speak its truth. Silence may conceal a love beyond measure, But a heart in turmoil will soon find its treasure."

Chandan Malana

Silent Support and Passionate Love: The Gift of Memories

My dearest friend, my trusted confidant,

I need your silent support, please respond,

For in this journey of life's winding path,

Your company alone can ease my wrath.

In times of loneliness and despair,

Your presence alone can make me repair,

With you by my side, I feel less alone,

Together we can conquer any unknown.

Passionate love is your only gift,

In your embrace, my spirits uplift,

Your heart, my haven, where I find peace,

With you, my love, all worries cease.

I need only your memories to live,

For in them, I find the love you give,

Each cherished moment a treasure to hold,

In your love, I find warmth in the cold.

I propose to you, my love, today,

To stand by me come what may,

In joy and sorrow, in highs and lows,

Together, our love will forever grow.

Let's walk this path, hand in hand,

Together, we will conquer every demand,

With you as my companion, my friend,

All hardships we can successfully bend.

In your eyes, I find my reflection,

In your smile, I see perfection,

Your love is my only salvation,

Together, we'll build a beautiful foundation.

My dearest love, will you be mine?

For in your love, I forever shine,

Let's embark on this journey of life,

Together, as companions, husband, and
wife.

Chandan Malana

Quote 36

" A companion in silence, my solace in strife, Your love is a fire that invigorates my life. Silent support is what I seek, for in your company I find peace. Passionate love, your only gift, memories of you, my heart uplift."

Chandan Malana

Sky Beneath Your Feet

My love for you is boundless and true,

Should I shout it from the mountaintops too?

If you say the word, I'll make it known,

I'll sing it out and make it shown.

I'll write it in the stars up high,

And paint it in the colors of the sky,

I'll shout it out for all to hear,

And make it known that you're my dear.

Should I tell the world about our love?

A love that's pure and sent from above,

I'll let them know, you are my heart,

And we'll never be too far apart.

My love for you is endless and strong,

A love that will never do you wrong,

Should I spread the news across the land?

And let the world know, I'm your biggest
fan.

I'll shout it out in every street,

And make it known, our love is sweet,

I'll sing it loud, with every breath,

And propose to you, until my death.

You are the one that I adore,

And I'll never love anyone more,

Should I tell the world about our bliss?

And propose to you, with every kiss.

I'll spread the sky under your feet,

And make you feel complete,

Our love will last forevermore,

And I'll propose, to the one I adore.

So let me know, if I should tell,

And spread the news of our love so well,

I'll shout it out, and make it known,

That you're the one, I want to call my own.

Chandan Malana

Quote 37

"My love for you knows no bounds, and if you give me the chance to share it with the world, I'll spread the sky under your feet with every proclamation of my devotion. Unbounded love, a promise to keep, With you, the sky's not the limit, it's where we leap."

Chandan Malana

Thirsty Heart's New Hope

My love, you are my shining light,

The one who makes my world so bright,

Without you, I was lost and low,

But now, with you, I bloom and grow.

You are the hope that keeps me strong,

The melody to my life's song,

My heart beats fast with every thought,

Of you, my love, who can't be bought.

You are the thirst I can't quench,

The only one I want to wrench,

Into my arms, to hold so tight,

And love you until morning's light.

My heart seeks you so impatiently,

Longing for you so desperately,

Hoping that you'll come my way,

And make my life complete each day.

In this journey of life we share,

I hope you'll take my hand and care,

For me, as I do for you,

Together, we can make dreams come true.

You are the missing puzzle piece,

That makes my life feel so complete,

With you, I know I'll find my way,

And never will I go astray.

My love, will you walk with me,

Through life's joys and sorrows, we'll see,

Together, we'll build a love so true,

A love that's meant for just us two.

So my love, with all my heart,

I ask you now, please never depart,

Will you be mine forevermore,

And make all my dreams and hopes soar?

Chandan Malana

Quote 38

"You are the beacon of hope that illuminates my life's path, the thirst that I constantly crave, the missing puzzle piece that completes my heart's desires. My heart yearns for you, and in this life, I search for nothing else but your love."

Chandan Malana

Through Life's Storms

If you'll be by my side for all time,

And hold me close when mountains climb,

If you'll forgive my faults and flaws,

And love me back without a pause,

If you'll walk with me through stormy seas,

And give me strength when I'm on my
knees,

If you'll be my shelter in the rain,

And fill my heart with joy again,

If you'll share with me life's highs and lows,

And be the wind beneath my wings that
blows,

If you'll be the sun that warms my soul,

And make me feel forever whole,

If you'll be my partner through thick and
thin,

And make my heart beat fast within,

If you'll be my lover and my friend,

And stay with me until the end,

Then I propose with all my heart,

That we should never be apart,

That we should join our lives together,

In love that will last forever,

I offer you my hand and heart,

And vow to never be apart,

To cherish you with all my might,

And hold you close both day and night,

Together we can conquer all,

And rise above life's bitter squall,

Together we can make a home,

Where love and happiness can roam,

So if you'll stay with me for life,

And be my partner through all strife,

Then please accept my love so true,

And let me spend my life with you.

Chandan Malana

Quote 39

"True love is not just about staying together for a lifetime, it's about holding hands during difficult times, forgiving each other's mistakes, and loving each other unconditionally."

Chandan Malana

Tongue Confessed

These eyes did wrong, they stole a glance

Though we had promised to keep our stance

Silent vows were shattered by this tongue

That spoke too soon and let our secret rung

The fault lies with these wayward eyes

That couldn't resist the tempting prize

Of stealing looks that were not meant to be

And breaking the silence so carelessly

In these eyes, the guilt does reside

For their desire could not be denied

They sought a glimpse, a stolen pleasure

And caused a breach in our hidden treasure

The fault was mine, but also theirs

These eyes that couldn't resist their snares

And the tongue that betrayed our pact

And let our secret slip, a regretful fact

Oh, how I wish these eyes were blind

And this tongue, more faithful and kind

To keep our secrets safe and sound

And not let them be lost, never to be found

These eyes, they wander and deceive

While this tongue can't help but relieve

The burden of secrets, it carries within

And expose our hidden sins

But now we must face the consequence

Of our mistakes and our lack of defense

Against the temptation of stolen glances

And the betrayal of our sacred advances

Let us learn from our faults and mistakes

And never again let our secrets break

Let us keep our promises, stay true and strong

And never let our eyes and tongue do us wrong.

Chandan Malana

Quote 40

"Eyes that betray the heart's deep desire, A tongue that reveals forbidden fire. The fault was in these eyes, which secretly sat to have a glimpse. We had vowed to remain silent, but this unfaithful tongue confessed."

Chandan Malana

Transcending Language: The Blessing Of Love

Transcending language, a blessing from above,

Love's essence beyond words, an eternal love,

Words may fail us, but love remains,

A language of the heart that forever sustains.

From different tongues, cultures, and lands,

Love unites us with its gentle hands,

Breaking down walls of fear and hate,

It transcends all boundaries, love conquers
fate.

A wordless language, yet it speaks volumes,

It elevates our souls, and our hearts it
consumes,

It binds us in a way that nothing else can,

Love's blessing, the foundation of every
man.

In love, we find solace and peace,

It's a language that can never cease,

It gives us wings, it helps us fly,

Love's blessing, our forever ally.

It's a language that brings us together,

A bond that will last forever,

It's the essence of our being,

Love's blessing, the reason for our seeing.

It transcends all earthly desires,

In love, we find what truly inspires,

It's a language that knows no bounds,

Love's blessing, the sweetest sound.

It's a language that needs no translation,

It speaks to every heart in every nation,

It brings hope, it brings light,

Love's blessing, our eternal sight.

Let us embrace this language of love,

It's a blessing that comes from above,

Let us transcend all earthly things,

Love's blessing, the joy that it brings.

Chandan Malana

Quote 41

"Love's blessing transcends the limits of
language, for it speaks to the heart and
soul in a way that words never could.
Beyond words and tongues, love's embrace,
A blessing divine, a sacred space."

Chandan Malana

Trust In Me, My Love

My dear, please trust in me with all your heart,

For I promise to love you with every part,

My desire is simple, it's not too much,

To make you mine, my love, with each loving touch.

Let our love blossom like a rose in bloom,

With every passing day, our hearts entwined
will groom,

I'll cherish you, my love, for all eternity,

Together we'll create a love story, pure and
lovely.

I'll hold your hand through every storm and
strife,

And be your guiding light through the
darkest of life,

We'll face every challenge, hand in hand,

Together we'll walk on this journey so
grand.

My love, I offer my heart and soul to you,

With all my being, my love will forever be
true,

I promise to cherish and adore you,

For there's no one else I want but you.

Let us dance in the moonlight, and under
the stars,

Let us embrace our love, without any scars,

I want to spend every moment with you,

And show you how much I love and adore
you.

My love, will you give me the chance,

To be your forever partner in this dance,

I'll be your rock, your everything,

Together we'll make our hearts sing.

My love, I propose to you with all my heart,

To be with me, and never to be apart,

Let us start this journey of love,

And take every step, hand in glove.

So, my dear, will you be mine,

To cherish, love and forever entwine,

Let our love story begin,

And let our hearts forever win.

Chandan Malana

Quote 42

"Trust me with your heart and I'll make you mine, For all I desire is to love you every moment, divine. Grant me your trust, let love be our guide, Forever together, our hearts intertwined."

Chandan Malana

Trying To Halt

Attempting to halt memories, a futile feat,

Reasoning with the heart, a fruitless treat,

When I try to banish thoughts of you,

My heartbeat seizes, bid adieu.

Yet I cannot resist reminiscing,

Your image in my mind persisting,

So I hold onto you as a lifeline,

An excuse to continue, to shine.

Your absence haunts me day and night,

But your memories fill me with delight,

I cling to them, a source of joy,

Happiness they never fail to deploy.

I know I should let go and move on,

But my heart is stubborn, like a fawn,

It yearns for you, day and night,

Refusing to give up without a fight.

I've tried to escape this endless loop,

To find new love, to find a troop,

But nothing compares to what we had,

My heart is forever chained, driving me
mad.

I long to forget, to be free,

From this love that's drowning me,

But memories don't fade, they persist,

Holding me captive, their hold so tight,
almost like a twist.

I've come to realize that letting go,

Is harder than I thought, the pain seems to
grow,

So I'll keep you in my heart and mind,

An excuse to keep living, to grind.

As the sun rises and sets each day,

I'll hold onto memories, come what may,

For though you're gone, you're never far,

My excuse to live, my shining star.

Chandan Malana

Quote 43

"Attempting to forget memories is like trying to halt a river's flow - futile and exhausting. The heart is stubborn and refuses to heed logic or reason. For me, attempting to forget you only halts my very existence. That's why I hold onto your memories as an excuse to live."

Chandan Malana

Unbreakable Bond: A Promise Renewed

A promise once made, now broken in two

But memories remain, both happy and blue

It's not a fault, to reminisce and recall

The moments we shared, the good times and all

I try not to think of you, but it's no use

Your place in my heart, it's just too huge

It's not possible to just move on and forget

The love that we had, and the moments we
met

Perhaps it's fate, that we are apart

But it doesn't mean, you're not in my heart

I still feel your presence, your love and your
care

Even if we're apart, it's something we share

I know I've made mistakes, I've let you down

But I'm still here, and I'm still around

I'm proposing to you, my love and my friend

To make amends, and let our love mend

Let's not dwell on the past, it's time to move
on

Together we'll face, the dawn of a new dawn

We'll create new memories, and start afresh

Our love will blossom, and never regress

Breaking promises, it's not what we intend

But life happens, and it's time to amend

Let's hold each other's hand, and make a
vow

To love each other, forever and now

Sometimes love needs, a second chance

To heal the wounds, and enhance romance

Let's give it a shot, and see where it leads

Our love will grow, and fulfill our needs

So here I am, proposing once more

To love you, to cherish you, forevermore

Let's break the shackles, of the past and move ahead

Our love is strong, and nothing to dread.

Chandan Malana

Quote 44

"Promises may fade away like morning dew, But memories of you, forever bright and true. A place in my heart, you'll forever claim, Even without thinking of you, it remains the same."

Chandan Malana

Unspoken Love, Unforgotten Name

Don't accuse my heart of weakness,

It's love that's made it helpless,

Though you don't speak my name,

My heart still burns with the same flame.

You think I've forgotten you,

But that's a false belief, it's true,

For every breath I take in life,

I remember you, my love, my wife.

My heart's beating to a different tune,

It sings of love that's never immune,

To the charms that you possess,

And the way you make my heart confess.

I know that things have been rough,

And our relationship's been tough,

But I propose that we give it one more chance,

And let our love's flame reignite and dance.

Let's forget the misunderstandings of the past,

And let our love's light shine bright and last,

For I cannot imagine my life without you,

And all my heart's desires, they're all for you.

You are the one who brings me joy,

And my heart's deepest sorrows you can destroy,

Together we can conquer all that life may bring,

And our love can be the strongest thing.

So let's take a leap of faith and start anew,

And let our love flourish and bloom like dew,

For I promise to love you more each day,

And cherish you forever, in every way.

Don't blame my heart's helplessness,

For it beats only for you, with tenderness,

So take my hand, and let's start anew,

For my heart belongs to you, my love, it's true.

Chandan Malana

Quote 45

"Blame not my heart for its helpless state, Remember me always, even nameless fate. Misunderstood, but I never forgot, Each breath I take whispers of you, my love-filled plot."

Chandan Malana

Waiting For Love's Touch

No soul has graced my eyes and touched my
heart,

No sailor on a ship, nor a life-long
sweetheart,

The stones claim that I've been adored by a
lover,

But I'm untouched wax, an unclaimed
treasure trove to discover.

The stars in the sky twinkle and gleam,

But I've not met anyone in whom I can
dream,

The sea's waves crash and roar with a
mighty roar,

Yet, no one has sailed into my heart's shore.

The roses in the garden bloom and sway,

But no one has stayed long enough to make
me stay,

The birds chirp and sing in sweet harmony,

But no melody compares to a love story.

The sun shines bright, bringing warmth to
my skin,

But no one's warmth compares to the love
within,

The moon shines bright, casting light on my
way,

But no one's light has shown me a lover's
display.

The mountains stand tall, sturdy and
strong,

But no one's strength has made me feel I
belong,

The valleys below, lush and green,

But no one's love has ever been seen.

The wind blows softly, whispering secrets to
me,

But no one's words have ever made my
heart free,

The rain falls gently, tapping on my roof,

But no one's love has ever been my true
proof.

The world spins round, day in and day out,

But my heart still waits, without any doubt,

That one day, my lover will come and
propose,

And in his arms, my heart will find repose.

So I wait patiently, hoping for a sign,

That one day, my love will make me shine,

For I am the wax, waiting to be touched,

By a love that's pure and true, never
rushed.

Chandan Malana

Quote 46

"Though stones whisper of love, my heart remains still, No traveler has entered, leaving my soul to fill, Untouched like wax, waiting for the one, Whose touch will ignite passion and love to come undone."

Chandan Malana

When Words Fail To Convey: Understand Our Silence

Our love for them is a sweet affliction,

We long to confess with great conviction,

But forced to keep it locked inside,

As though our hearts must always hide.

Why can't they see what's in our hearts,

As we struggle to keep love's darts,

Our silence is not a lack of care,

But a sign of the depths we dare.

Is it so vital to speak love's words,

Or can actions show like singing birds,

Our devotion shines in what we do,

It's a truth that will always ring true.

Yet society demands we declare,

That we must make our feelings bare,

But some emotions run too deep,

For words alone to fully keep.

Love isn't a game of show and tell,

It's a bond that weaves its spell,

With every action, every touch,

It's a feeling that can mean so much.

So let us not be judged by words,

But by the love that truly stirs,

Deep within our hearts and souls,

That guides us and makes us whole.

For love is not just what we say,

It's the love we give every day,

In our actions and in our deeds,

That fulfills all our loving needs.

Let our love speak without a sound,

In every smile, in every round,

Of gentle touch and warm embrace,

Our love is present in every place.

Chandan Malana

Quote 47

"Expressions of love go beyond the tongue, Actions and silence, where its truest form is sung. For love is not just the words we say, But the deeds we do each and every day. Love's truest expression lies not in the words we speak, but in the actions we take and the silence we keep."

Chandan Malana

Wrapped In Love: Enraptured By Your Beauty

With every blink, I see your face

And longing for your warm embrace

I want to make you my forever

And love you like no other ever

Wrapped around your loving arms

Is where I feel most safe from harm

Your beauty shines both in and out

And fills my world with joy and clout

You are the epitome of grace

I want to see your smiling face

In every moment of my life

To cherish you as my loving wife

I'll make you feel like royalty

And shower you with loyalty

Together we will make our way

Through life's journey day by day

You light up every room you're in

And fill my heart with joy within

I want to hold you close and tight

And make every day feel so right

With every breath that I take

I know that our love won't break

I want to make you mine for good

And cherish you like a lover should

I promise to be there for you

In everything we say and do

Together we will conquer all

And make each other's hearts enthrall

So my love, I must propose

To be with you, my heart explodes

Let's make each other's dreams come true

And spend our lives just me and you.

Chandan Malana

Quote 48

"Your beauty, a vision, an eternal delight, With every blink, my world ignites. Embrace me always, your love holding tight, Now and forever, you're the one I'll never let out of sight."

Chandan Malana

Yearning Hearts: Love Amidst Separation

Amidst thc time of separation's pain,

We long for you, our hearts remain

Restless, with every passing day,

Our love for you won't fade away.

Our circumstances leave us feeling weak,

As we yearn for the comfort that you speak,

Helpless, we struggle to hold on,

To the love that we've cherished all along.

Just read our eyes, and you will see,

The depths of love we hold for thee,

For even though we must be apart,

Our love for you will never depart.

We cannot deny the truth we feel,

Our love for you is so very real,

But circumstances can make it tough,

And sometimes, it feels like it's just not enough.

Our hearts are torn, and our souls are pained,

Yet, our love for you will remain unchanged,

For even though we are apart,

We hold onto the love that's in our heart.

We cannot change the way things are,

But we know that our love will go far,

For even though we are apart,

Our love will continue to grow in our heart.

Our love for you is strong and true,

And we know that it's the same for you,

For even though we must be apart,

Our love will always stay in our heart.

So, though the time of separation makes us restless,

And our circumstances make us helpless,

We want you to know, without a doubt,

That our love for you will always shout.

Chandan Malana

Quote 49

"Separation's agony knows no bounds, But love speaks louder without a sound. Eyes, the windows to a love so deep, Through the pain and helplessness, they'll forever speak."

Chandan Malana

Your Lovely Face Is My Heart's Sole Image

My heart's sole image is your lovely face,

In your warm embrace, I find my solace and grace.

Without you, my world is incomplete,

With your love, my heart feels replete.

Needing you more than the world, my love,

I cannot imagine my life without you
thereof.

You are the reason for my every breath,

With you by my side, I fear no death.

My heart belongs to you, my sweet,

Your love makes my life complete.

I offer you my heart with no reservation,

In your loving arms, I find salvation.

A love beyond the world we share,

Our bond is rare, beyond compare.

With you, I want to spend eternity,

Together, we will conquer destiny.

My darling, let me be your forever,

I promise to leave you never.

In good times and bad, I'll be by your side,

Our love will forever abide.

Let's walk the path of love together,

Our hearts beating as one forever.

With each passing moment, my love grows,

For you, my heart overflows.

My heart's desire is to make you mine,

Together, we will shine and brightly shine.

I'll be your rock, your shelter, and your
guide,

Our love, a forever-treasured tide.

So my dear, will you take my hand,

And walk with me through life's vast land?

Together, we can make our dreams come true,

My heart belongs to you, and only you.

Chandan Malana

Quote 50

"Your face, a lovely image in my heart, I need you more than any world apart. My heart belongs to you, my love, Burning bright, like the stars above. Within my heart, your visage pure, An image cherished, love secure, More than the world, I long for thee, Our love transcends, boundless and free."

Chandan Malana

Buy Me A Cup Of Coffee

Dear readers,

Thank you so much for taking the time to read my words. If I have in some way managed to touch your life, then I am truly honoured.

I hope that my poetry and words have been able to time travel you back to any emotion and in some way, some where, somehow, in some place, in some moment touched your life then my life has become purposeful for others.

If you have enjoyed my work and
would like to show your
appreciation, I would be delighted
if you could buy me a cup of coffee.
Your support would mean the
world to me. Every bit helps and I
am truly grateful for your
generosity. Thank you once again,

Your faithful writer

**Chandan
Malana**

Paytm, Google pay, Phonepe, UPI

chandan.malana@paytm

******

paypal.me/ChandanMalana

******

chandanmalana@gmail.com

******

instagram.com/chandan_malana

******

EUR account details

Account holder: Chandan Malana
SWIFT/BIC: TRWIBEB1XXX
IBAN: BE75 9674 9601 8051
Wise's address:
Avenue Louise 54, Room S52
Brussels
1050
Belgium

******

GBP account details

GBP Outside the UK

Account holder: Chandan Malana
SWIFT/BIC: TRWIGB2L
IBAN: GB71 TRWI 2314 7012 4893 22
Wise's address:
56 Shoreditch High Street
London
E1 6JJ
United Kingdom

GBP Inside the UK

Account holder: Chandan Malana
Sort code: 23-14-70
Account number: 12489322
IBAN: GB71 TRWI 2314 7012 4893
22
Wise's address:
56 Shoreditch High Street
London
E1 6JJ
United Kingdom

****

USD account details

Account holder: Chandan Malana
ACH and Wire routing number:
084009519
Account number:
9600010468802671
Account type: Checking
Wise's address:
30 W. 26th Street, Sixth Floor
New York NY 10010
United States

******

BSC
BNB Smart Chain
[BEP20]

0x652347bc8ccbe876a1cd93534a1
8c6d4b7bd4d8f

Books By This Author

Rainbow Of Emotions

50 River Beneath 50 Ocean

Promises Of Mine

Vol. 2

www.ingramcontent.com/pod-product-compliance
Lightning Source LLC
Chambersburg PA
CBHW061333250726

48657CB00004B/1144